Praise for *The Gardens of Our Childhoods*

In *The Gardens of Our Childhoods* John Belk transfers the Bard's comment that "All the world's a stage" from the theater's stage to the comic, violent, vulnerable, and wild ring of WrestleMania. This is a book of searching, tender, open, moments. Life is beautiful but not without its dangers. Belk knows this is true and does a fine job guiding us down the garden path.

—Matthew Dickman, author of *Wonderland*

To say that the bulk of these splendid poems is about pro wrestling is to say that Robert Frost wrote mainly about sound agricultural practices. When John Belk says that seeing a gladiator's spectacular move is like being kissed unexpectedly by someone you have a crush on, he reminds us how life and art and sport work: we script them to the degree we can, yet there's always a surprise. No matter who we are, our dreams are what unite us, for everything we do is about "coming together / & leaving," about hoping "to be known, to / be touched, to be less lonely than before."

—David Kirby, author of *Help Me, Information*

With the pageantry of professional wrestling as his lens and southern American boyhood as his vantage, John Belk shows us "something beautiful / made by a boy with all his heart" in his earnest, dazzling debut collection. *The Gardens of Our Childhoods* charts the slim line between masculine strength and vulnerability, asking us what it means for—and costs—this collection's vast cast of characters to commit to tenderness in a world waiting to stomp on their backs and toss them out of the ring. After all, "who would expect a large man born of noonsun & sinew to be delicate"? Belk powerfully summons legendary pro wrestlers, communes with their families, and invokes his own beloveds in a book that moves deftly between the spectacle of stage makeup and the quiet of newly planted irises: beauty performed and beauty deliberately tended to.

—Rachel Mennies, author of *The Naomi Letters*

THE GARDENS OF OUR CHILDHOODS

JOHN BELK

AUTUMN
HOUSE PRESS

THE GARDENS OF OUR CHILDHOODS
An Autumn House Book

ISBN: 978-1-637680-35-3   LCCN: 2021950319

For information about permission to reprint, contact:

Autumn House Press
5530 Penn Avenue
Pittsburgh, PA 15206
www.autumnhouse.org

"Autumn House Press" and "Autumn House" are registered trademarks owned by Autumn House Press, a nonprofit corporation whose mission is the publication and promotion of poetry and other fine literature.

Autumn House Press receives state arts funding support through a grant from the Pennsylvania Council on the Arts, a state agency funded by the Commonwealth of Pennsylvania, and the National Endowment for the Arts, a federal agency.

This project is supported in part by an award from the National Endowment for the Arts. To find out more about how National Endowment for the Arts grants impact individuals and communities, visit www.arts.gov.

For Mom and Dad

Table *of* Contents

With the great gale we journey
     That breathes from gardens thinned,
Borne in the drift of blossoms
     Whose petals throng the wind.

          —A. E. Housman, "The Merry Guide"

Trash

My allotment
at the garden
used to fill
with flotsam:
bottles, paper
towels, knives,
an empty
can of beer.

In 1997 Hulk
Hogan turned
heel. The fans
threw trash,
chili dogs &
spoiled milk &
pilsner—
piloried rage just

like every year
at Thanksgiving
when Uncle,
sad-voiced
& serious would
say: *aren't you
too old for this
wrestling trash?*

& isn't that
a metaphor:
every thin relationship
& fallen hero,
trash &
a garden, wrestling,
Hollywood Hogan &
holiday dinners at home.

Perry Saturn makes ends meet after a failed tour with New Japan Pro-Wrestling

In the solar fields past Barstow
Perry collects birds. Every

morning, stimmed & unconcerned
he wears a welder's apron & work

boots, walks among panels 2
hours at a time scooping remains

of avian frames caught between
tower & ground. He smells of

cedar & earth, pungent body oil
& leather & salt. Each bird

is a cloud at the edge of
apocalypse—carbon-black, lit

with fire. Perry scoops them into
buckets, carries them off.

Each one, he thinks,
is a sorry metaphor.

∼

Perry takes lunch on a support girder of Ivanpah
Solar Tower 2, carefully unwraps a dry turkey club

with tomato. The plant powers two telescopes &
half the golden valley. Underground are solenoids

& valves—tanks of molten salt that store the sun.
This is what a star looks like up close.

～

Perry puts the remains of a California
gull in his bucket. One of its eyes is still

knowable, its burnt breast wearing the
bulk of its trauma. For a moment he

wants to return it to the beach, dip it
in the soft Pacific & be forgiven for

breaking his mother's heart. He shakes
the thought. In a bathroom that smells

of cooked meat & acetone he
re-ups & daydreams of high school

& a time when he wasn't lonely
& stardust & beach grit & flight

& some far-off future, some
other world of swirling color
& undivided light.

The Death of Owen Hart

here was a man beloved—even the worst in the business
mourned for Owen Hart. if a man has enemies in life

they are often buried by death, but Owen made genuine
sorrow grow from the most hardpacked of soil. I was a

melancholy boy for sure, but loved, so I suppose I relate. it
seems that life is a pity's wheel for losing, especially for

melancholy boys—losing coins, loved ones, a thimble of
resolve. I lost my language once, drunk. I lost lovers, no more

or less than most, & friends. when I was very small I lost
a tin man in the dirt beneath my mother's favorite tree.

how much have I lost? & how? sitting in my garden shoveling
turnips into buckets for the winter. & how should I mourn:

one more fallen, stunted, rolled aside to the fallow edge
where stone becomes grass & beyond, a host of mothers

singing, their voices carried in endless open fields.

Buff Bagwell's Mother

Buff Bagwell's mother sold her condo in Marietta,
Georgia, through an utterly average real estate
brokerage getting above market value. After months
of learning Dutch she bought a flat in Bruges
one flight up from a jazz club named The Duke.
Incurably smart, she drinks coffee with chicory &
writes to her son weekly. His fingertips still tingle but
he can breathe on his own & walk again. Below her
the sound of a gravelly stand-up bass floats through
refurbished flooring. She flexes her calves a bit,
stretches, does a subtle échappé to the window &
practices her French: Qu'est-ce que tu vas faire?

incantation [*Fraxinus ornus*]

in this ring I rest
under a moment
of cloud

the Meliae were born of the blood
that fell on Gaia when Cronus
castrated Uranus   they nursed
the infant Zeus   feeding him
goat's milk & honey   some say
the spine of the world is an   ash
Yggdrasil   a Puritan prayer &   a
garden somewhere   a mountain
a mother   a father & a boy
a fight   & a hope that you're ok

John Belk

Perry Saturn fell in love with a mop

Perry bought a pair of linen curtains, too long
to dress the sliding glass door. he thought
he was in love with them. he once loved
a turtle. a fish. the ocean on its side
when it was sleeping. he loved a girl, a few
even, but never like the first. he loves better
now—still, there are breaths we cannot
keep: another heart opens for a time
& we bathe soft in another life,
tangled in curtains, carmine tressed &
a tart curl of lip, oyster freckled, happy.
we dance with a painted mophead like an
ancient fool, a wrestler, a well-dressed open
glass door inviting us into the day.

The Cauliflower Alley Club

Ricky Steamboat & Nick Bockwinkel & Ivan Koloff share
drinks at the bar of the *RMS Queen Mary*, Long Beach
across the harbor like a dream. Wendi Richter & Joyce
Grable talk too loud about stealing Velvet McIntyre's
boot. She wrestled the rest of her career barefoot, had
the prettiest toes in the business. The Fabulous Freebirds
smoke in a corner while a waiter tries to explain that under
California law smoking indoors is prohibited, even on the
former Allied transport & retired flagship of the Cunard-
White Star Line. All the talk & booze is wholesome, kayfabe
off the portside for tonight. Nobody feels forgotten—even
Ole Anderson, wallowing in prefabricated bitterness & love.

Stasiak & Sammartino

I'll be the greatest heel on the green green earth
& he was

but how could anyone not love a lovely heart?

Stasiak & Sammartino II

Stasiak's finish
was called the Heart Punch—
an oversold thrust

to the sternum of
any damn unlucky fool
to go against the

Man. What a power,
to make the heart explode with
a touch—to burst

someone with joy at
a barbecue or horse track
or church, flooding each

living second with
gentle four-chambered delight.
Stasiak tried three

times to put it on
before the cock crowed &
Bruno laid him low

with a belly-to-
belly suplex to crown the
night. In the end

that's all it took: skin
to skin & grappled bodies
graced in might.

John Belk

The Gardens of Our Childhoods

It is a well-known fact that
wrestling is scripted—every
possible outcome laid bare,
gridded as a garden where
our gentle, childish breaths
skirt low growth of chamomile
& thyme. The sun is lifted
high, the whole wide world
a painted hero hoisting a near-
vanquished foe. We sit, hands
locked, knowing the ending,
still watching it fall.

Marcus Bagwell's Mother

I.

Marcus Bagwell's mother wanted nothing more than
for him to be a blessing unto the world. She named
him Marcus after the Flemish printmaker Marcus
Gheeraerts the Elder, whose 1 x 2 meter etching of
Bruges was said to have taken 10 full copper plates
& 2 years to complete. She found a print of it
in a thrift shop in Marietta, Georgia, for $7.35 &
hung it above the sofa where she swaddled Marcus
as an infant, dreaming of cobbled city centres &
varicose canals swollen with each year's thaw.

II.

In 1973, Marcus Bagwell's mother had her palm
read by a fortune-teller in Sarasota, Florida. The
meaning wasn't important—all spiritual chicanery
& fluffed-up abracadabrism—but the thought:
Ms. Bagwell, incurably smart, visiting a fortune-
teller for no good reason. She happened to be in
the neighborhood with several hours free, having
just been let go from her job at the optometrist's
office, but also having paid in advance for the full
month of daycare which lasted until 5 p.m. The
waiting room was humid as she left, Persian rugs
uncomfortable over beachy hardwood floors &
Tommy Dorsey playing from an old turntable. She
thought of the medium's message & of Marcus at
daycare, photos of Sarasota literati along the walls:
Elvis, Cher, The Allman Brothers Band, & Cecil B.

DeMille. She let the screen door close on rattled salt-
worn hinges & stepped into the blinding south
Florida sun.

III.

When she was 38, Marcus Bagwell's mother married
a park foreman. He was diligent & unambitious,
content with an expanded cable package & wife
& a stepson who by this point was developing
a young man's body & aptitude for men's things
like baseball & fighting. Ms. Comfrey née Bagwell
gave her son boxing gloves for his 14th birthday. Her
husband sparred with him twice.

IV.

Ms. Bagwell left her husband amicably after 3
years & moved back to Marietta. Marcus, 17 &
a man in his own right, took a job at a water park, a
lumberyard, a boxing gym. Marcus Bagwell's mother
looked at her son with a mother's love & thought
how much we are the sum of our labors: quartersawn
logs & golden gloves & slide rivets & beautiful
sons, gestated flesh, at once our own flesh & not.

V.

The first girl Marcus loved besides his mother was
Lucy DiMartino. They had homeroom together
& Marcus liked that her hair smelled of Valencia
orange & vanilla. Ms. Bagwell drove them to the
cinema where they kissed for the first time in the
back row of Norman Jewison's *Moonstruck*. Marcus
thought the movie was boring except for Olympia
Dukakis, who reminded him of his own mother.

That night on the drive home, Ms. Bagwell saw in
the rearview mirror as Marcus brushed Lucy's hand
cautiously, so unsure of himself but happy. She hoped
to all breath he could feel like that forever.

VI.

Marcus Bagwell's mother did not expect him to
become a wrestler. In her youth she held his infant
form under her 1562 map of Bruges & thought he
might play jazz, breed exotic cats, maybe own a cafe
that sold virgin lime rickeys & artisan grilled cheese
to tourists. She named each sandwich in her mind,
clever names like "Lingonberry & Lacey Swiss" or
"Gooey Gamonéu with Roasted Cashew." Marcus
first teamed with 2 Cold Scorpio, whose real name
was Charlie Scaggs & who had visited Bruges once
during a booze-soaked stint in the European indies.
In late '93 they won the WCW tag belts before
Scorpio left for Korea. Ms. Bagwell was sad that
Marcus didn't go, missing the cherry blossoms
of Jinhae-gu along the Yeojwacheon stream.

VII.

Marcus Bagwell changed his name to Buff in late '96
after an NWO heel turn. Buff loved himself in a way
that made Marcus uncomfortable but famous. His
mother was happy that he was happy, & he bought
her Turkish coffee with chicory & Tommy Dorsey
records & all the things that made her heart glad
to exist in such a difficult, difficult world. At a house
show in Tampa, Buff was slated to job to Johnny
Swinger but didn't, instead catching a SuperSaver
shuttle an hour south where he got drunk on a

private Sarasota beach & wrote a poem about
Lucy DiMartino, who he hadn't seen in 11
years & who he heard was happily married
to the owner of a flooring showroom in South
Carolina that catered to low-cost vacation rentals.

VIII.

When Buff Bagwell broke his spine, his mother
rushed to the hospital in a 2006 Toyota Celica
with a bag of toiletries & several changes of
clothes. Ms. Bagwell had been disappointed with
Buff's womanizing persona & his real-life work
as a gigolo, but even so she loved her son whose
muscled body lay wrapped in feeding tubes &
drip lines & cords to power the many machines
helping him to breathe. She thought it unfair that
a mother should outlive her son, especially when
he still hadn't been to Bruges & all she could think
in that moment was of the places she wanted him
to call from at 2 a.m. Marietta time to talk about the
nice man he sat beside on the plane & the airport
grilled cheese that tasted exactly like hers & the
blossoms at Jinhae, just unfurling, outer petals
falling after a cool Korean breeze.

letterlocking

to crease the page
crevasse across

filamented skin
the body of a word

back-of-the-envelope
bitterness

how the pome of
a stone fruit

feels like the end
of a sword

John Belk

Angle of Regard

the best angles in wrestling
come out of nowhere: Scott
Hall waltzing from the

crowd, toothpick on his
lip & a shit-eating bad
guy grin. it's like the

first time someone kissed
you—how she caught you off
guard in the moonlight out-

side of your parents' house.
how the persimmon smell
blown up off her neck was

a leaf strung taut in a tree
made for climbing. how
every moment of hurt

the next twenty years
would float in that tree,
pulled up, up into a

warm Sunday night
in the northernest part
of north Louisiana &

you, just there, sixteen
shit-eating grin, knowing
nothing of another

person's heart. how each
person's heart is a tree, ever,
& growing & galled to the

touch. how sometimes,
from the right angle,
under the right shape

of moon, when the air
smells slight of persimmon
you can see so far.

a business without heart or conscience

the way we know to grasp for milk,
vocalize need into air, dream. long
before we held each other in
safe moments of daybreak was
the knowledge of binding rope,
a made pot, sharing life with a dog.
the scream of the murdered &
murderer, both, tremble through
100-year pines conjuring our dominion.
it's just not going right. for every love
is a backwards glance, a man grappled
with another in struggle, a spectacle,
burlesque, the ritual of our deepest,
oldest bones.

Hermeneutics (that we should fly)

It is 10 ft from the top of the ring post
to the floor. It is 100,000 AU to the far
edge of the solar system. It is infinite,
the space between hearts. All of this
life is searching, flight: coming together
& leaving, grappling air. We soar
between body & margin, carrying
meaning with a hope: to be known, to
be touched, to be less lonely than before.
We entwine & disentangle, throw
ourselves from turnbuckles to agony
below. Hermes used the caduceus to
separate warring snakes. But I worry:
what if snakes grow friendless after
being forced apart? & what if all our
struggle is the best that we can do?

bar trivia: good things have to happen to some-one

(it is a statistical likelihood)

(like goldfinches in the garden or
chervil bottoming out, wilting in midday sun)
(even a bad push can turn good) (the crowd
                loves a heel as much as a face
because why be alive

save the chance of buttercream, a black eye,
lemon & interlaced fingers
                after an evening at a show)

(good things have to happen to someone: there is
no good reason not)

WrestleMania XVI & suicide

When the Fabulous Moolah pulled Kat from the ring
behind Val Venis's back I thought I would die. The injustice

of it all: that evil always wins, underhanded & impossible to
reconcile with hope. It's a passion play slumping to Summer-

Slam to be born. The cruelest moments of our lives are laced
in white boots, a fist full of somas at the Jaffa Shrine & maybe

we'll sleep through to Macon.

John Belk

Stone Cold Steve Austin's Mother

she thought from the moment he
was born that his head looked like
a podger[1]   beautiful & asymmetric
keen as a book of birds   she
spent most of the 12-hour labor
pretending she was at sea   perched
in the nest of an old British sloop
the whole sky unfurled to the
bleeding edge of tomorrow   afloat
in her mind she thought of all
the boy might do one day   the harm
& delight   the various ports of
call   atop her 3-masted ship-
of-war & just as the Pirate Queens
of Old[2]   she wished him life : no
regrets   all champagne & daybreak
a world of inevitable pain   good
mince pie for the long   difficult years
a bit of luck & a following wind

---

1   a remnant piece of dough used for making the filling cavities in
       traditional pie-&-mash fare

2   Teuta; Æthelflæd; Sayyida al Hurra; 鄭一嫂; Charlotte Badger; Anne
       Bonny; Sadie the Goat; Jeanne de Clisson, the Lioness of Brittany;
       Jacquotte Delahaye; Anne Dieu-le-Veut; Ingela Olofsdotter
       Gathenhielm

definition of the continental shelf

n. the segment of ocean floor ownable
by men   where light still travels
cookie-sweet & fading   all energy &
flamboyance   a crown of thorns
we've had since we were young

the man says survivors are always happy
because at least they are alive   they sing
their songs   tell tales of their hurt
give it a spine & feed it   ragged
on floors of silent seas

the man says slavery is in little things
a tea set from Saxony   cuff links   a sweetmeal
biscuit from Leeds   12 nautical miles
offshore is the farthest a nation can claim
beyond that :   the sum of all we can't hold

but shelves are curate   emancipate
meant to show & to tell   a bird feather
beads   the friend we hurt   a dream   meant
to scrawl our mark on the curve of the earth
to die with crumbs on our faces ;

The Undertaker's American Badass Phase

Sometime around the millennium Undertaker dropped
the undead phenom act   gone were the somber church
bells & howlings of pale Paul Bearer   instead he
rode a motorcycle   more human & destructible   there
was a feud with Kurt Angle where the ring was destroyed
by magic & another where Diamond Dallas Page stalked
the deadman's wife   & I get it—we're all
due for a change now & then   but life takes too much
to watch our great heroes   gradually warm to the touch

dead letter office

boxes of unopened
letters   daughters
who never go home it's
a junkyard of twirling
together   two legs &
a mystic river
gardens we'll never
know

bar trivia: no wrestler has ever used an Annie Lennox song as entry music

(if they had we would know such human capacity for love)
    (intimate breaths on a neck in
    moonlight, the name of a favorite doll)
    (because:
who would expect a large man, born of noonsun & sinew to be delicate)

(& who would hold his hand, a lengthened torch, cottage lace,
    a saw & a set of pastels, interrupted aster)

(no wrestler has ever used an Annie Lennox song as entry music
           for fear the whole world might weep, split
    apart at its belt, whistle its conscience to make itself cry)

Jimmy Snuka's Mother

There are moments when my life
escapes me—moments when I tried
to help it: shooed it through an open
window, unceremonious, like a june
bug or moth caught where it shouldn't.
There is no outside to God my friend says,
& in this moment we are all undone. In
this moment I am a Kashmiri elephant,
long extinct & a bank robber hiding
in the Badlands of Utah & a toddler
on the banks of the Neva River dipping
her feet in waters of azimuth-blue. How
many lives can we live & not under-
stand? Like how every great city is built
on a river. How there is no one answer to
evil in the world. How the angle between
us & a heavenly body is bluer than a bend
in the Kashmiri Black Jade where elephants
once watered their young. Or how so many
mothers must watch their sons go so
unforgivably wrong.

John Cena's Spinner Belt

who wouldn't love such a gaudy display of in-your-face be-fucking-better

poem about a dying mall

this is a poem about a dying mall.
its arteries clogged & hardening. the abercrombie

struggling. low footfall.
this is a poem about a collection of stores

falling apart. flagships failing. hearts beating
with more difficulty than before. short breath.

this is a poem about dying. phasing out.
collapsing under the weight.

Perry Saturn at a bed-&-breakfast in Katonah, New York, before a January sunrise

In the anxious morning
Perry wakes & thinks of:

1.   a lock of red hair

2.   three horses

3.   the time he saw her at Walmart after five years in Japan;
        he bought paint & canvasboard & talked of Katagami
        & the wet autumns of Akita Prefecture before the coming
        snow

4.   rookeries

5.   sweet machine smoke in the deserts above
        LA

6.   canyon fires & longing

7.   & how, of all the lives
        he imagines in the infinite multiverse of his heart
        there is one where he is with her

My love wants a chicken named Eleanor of Aquitaine

In dreams you forgive me the unspent years. You still
eat exactly three fig cakes & roll your eyes when I talk
about wrestling. You said when the pigs die we'll get
chickens, name one Eleanor of Aquitaine. I watch
you plant iris bulbs, hands breaking dirt as an egg.
I often do not think of you in daylight—a mistake
perhaps. I know you will be sat above a potter's wheel
or mashing blocks of coir into soil pulp for growing.
In dreams you forgive me all the men I could have been—

Razor Ramon

It's easy to say we all have choices—
sitting stoned, watching old wrestling vids
& listening to Mazzy Star & reading
YouTube comments about a guy who
named his heroin rig after Hope Sandoval
& how she never left his side or let him
down for 18 years & how he has been clean
since June 10, 2016. I am glad. It's hard
to explain how even at heights some of us
can't see past ourselves—how Razor Ramon
would always be the Bad Guy, even after his
face turn when everyone loved him but him.

Blackjack Mulligan's Mother

Blackjack was birthed in Sweetwater Tx to a
rattlesnake & a baker . Blackjack's mother taught
him how to make bread giving him rounds
of dough to roll & knead . Blackjack kept his
hands busy for idle hands are devils' playthings

Blackjack's mother's name was Sara . she made
love to a snake out of spite . her husband was a
drunkard & besides . snakes have pretty eyes but
cold & shriveled souls . Sara kept a locket of the
first woman she ever loved . she also had pretty eyes

Sara loved Blackjack with all her heart . he was a
gentle boy & large for his age . he dreamed of slender
fishing birds . herons . egrets . ibis . bitterns . he saw
a bittern once in an aviary in Old Laredo . it was sad
because aviaries are sad places especially in Old Laredo

& especially because bitterns breed in the marshes of
southern Canada . Sara was glad he got to see a bird
but sad that Blackjack was sad . it is a nice fact that
mothers can be sad for their sons especially sensitive
boys like Blackjack who get sad more often than most

so Blackjack would go through life loved by his
mother & sensitive . loving slender birds & bread
making . he would learn to wrestle to keep his hands
busy because kneading dough or muscles is basically
the same for a sensitive 300 lb man . & Sara would

think of him often & her drunken fuck of a husband
& the woman she truly loved & the pretty eyes of
a rattlesnake & all the ways a mother singing sounds
just like a bittern in Old Laredo : sad & slender-billed
full of thick-throated longing for far-off Canadian springs ;

The time Vince McMahon tore both his quadriceps while sliding angrily

into the ring at the Royal Rumble after a botched finish on live PPV

it wasn't supposed to happen like that: Batista & Cena were meant to
go over together, Batista hooking the top rope while Cena hit the mat

but few bits of life ever go according to plan—most days are destined
for creative use of school glue & gear tape & unplanned clotheslines

to lock in a spot at the WrestleMania main event. some days the refs—
bought & paid for from Vince's pocket—still get it wrong. these are

the days of injustice: all the young boys & girls beaten or maimed or
shot in the streets, pushed aside like ill-gotten memories & surrounded

by confusion, cut deep, muscles rolled half-way up their thighs

shipletters

the paper smells like
mutton, mint jelly, india
ink. a prize fighter,
he tears through a sentence
splitting the wafer seal.
the paper smells like
docks, magnesium &
weatherboarding, pine.
he once thought his father
like wildfire, brush.
he holds hands with a
woman he paid to fuck
& falls asleep for the night.
the paper smells like
tender shoots of grass
in the fading hours of
a hidden moon.

Madison Square

in the beginning The Garden was an ice rink leased to P. T.
Barnum . in 1898 Nikola Tesla demonstrated the first remote-
controlled robot to cheers & in 1925 the first ring debuted
in a light heavyweight bout between Berlenbach & Delaney

the first WrestleMania was held there too . Hulk Hogan & Mr. T
The Iron Sheik . O to be present for history : the roar of the crowd
an ocean on a far-away world . a palace . a grand purple desert
under pale-milk stars . why do we like a fight? the spectacle?

the violence on the floor? somewhere a mother holds her grown
son for the first time in many years . she braids his hair like he is 8
again . dreams of slowing time . somewhere a pulsar wind nebula
turns around a dying neutron star . a boy lifts weights in a garage

in south Georgia . draws pictures of things he can see in the sky
at night . in a garden somewhere everything folds together
a crowd erupts at a shooting star press . a man picks flowers
for his mother : fleeting & superluminal

> or something beautiful
> made by a boy with all his heart

Hacksaw Jim Duggan's Mother

The *Madonna del Cardellino* was given to Lorenzo Nasi as a wedding gift. He made love that night under her fluttered Sabine gaze—held his new wife asleep in the early hours of an unspectacular Florentine morning, the gentle rise of

her chest against his chest, her heart in tercets under a chiaroscuro outcropping of cloud. In 1548, Nasi's home was destroyed in an earthquake, the Madonna broken into 17 pieces, later put back together [poorly], & even later restored. Cardellino

means goldfinch, delicate in their own & off at once in a wanton freak, a whirl of chirpish chatter in the hand of a child lord. Nasi's wife eats honey & cheese, pane di segale & boiled rings from Puglia & the little green-yellow figs that look like

goldfinches, joking to her husband of the coincidence as she calls him to sleep. & he sleeps & dreams of Calabrian citrus & his mother's favorite bread & the way his wife's hand quivers when holding a well of blue Moroccan ink. In his dream the virgin

speaks in the voice of a rainstorm or a flitted goldfinch, the voice of his mother baking. She says: *Lorenzo, Lorenzo my son*—her chestnut hair lifted in gentle warbles by a sudden slight of breeze. He wakes, his wife held fast beside him in the unspectacular

Florentine morning, her chest rising softly & falling in tercets under a blue clouded chiaroscuro moon. Outside a cardellino is singing, somewhere. Of course they will die. But they are not afraid. There is so much softness in the early light of the world not to laugh. In 400 years a man will carry a 2" x 4", make his Catholic mother proud.

The Fingerpoke of Doom

the worst ending to a wrestling match ever shown on live tv; regularly credited
with the decline of World Championship Wrestling in the late 1990s; wherein the
title transferred back to Hollywood Hulk Hogan; wherein Kevin Nash proceeded
to clownishly lie down & allow himself to be pinned after a gentle poke to the
chest; wherein 600,000 viewers changed channels to watch Mick Foley win the
WWF Championship over The Rock in a No Disqualifications match on Monday
Night Raw, often cited as one of the best bouts of all time; wherein the entire
landscape of wrestling changed in a single, ill-conceived moment; wherein the
final television rating was a disappointing 5.0 & the best days of wrestling—like
all things worth loving—politely came to a close.

one two skip a few a hundred

i want the way alpine
dianthus smells of clove

& clumsy hand holding
& anise. i want a bed like

an overstuffed carnation
& a vintage bike that

rolls smooth, a real road
chopper. i want lasagna

& a chaise & a wood-
shop in the country that

i always mean to use but
never do. if i were better

i would raise chickens,
give eggs to the poor.

i want to be better.   i want to.
i want to hold an ancient river's hand.

bar trivia: Venice has been sinking for years

after Wisława Szymborska

(Venice seems to be infinitely under water—
Piazza San Marco daily rolling its trousers
to greet the morning tide) (offshore
       fish spawn in forests of laminaria,
       urchins crawl their haunts in a shuffle,
       a distant whale sounds a rounded call)

(*there is so much everything that nothing is hidden
quite nicely*—how sea air tastes of metal & oats,
a strained kiss, magnesium salts after snow
       how one heart finds another then
       moves on) (northward the four great
       basilicas prepare for a year of jubilee

their holy doors unwalled for pilgrims, some
small bit of pardon) (across the sea lovers fall
asleep, windows open to a cool Moroccan breeze
a man holds a woman on a waterfront in Sydney
the Yellow River floods & recedes & floods again)
       (there is something so natural about it all

or something so human, like
bringing someone joy in a quiet way)

       (a reminder:
that trouble isn't forever
that Venice has been sinking for years)

John Belk

Perry Saturn wonders

after all these years if
he could still buy a house
with a garden of petunias &
sunchoke & delphinium
sour cherry & Comtesse de
Bouchaud clematis along
the back cedar fence if
it is too late when the drugs
don't work to get a lily or
lisianthus build a life the way
it should have been only
now with half a liver &
a face tattoo & a brand new
person to love who looks
just like him but with
lavender gardenia eyes

Good Endings

we are drawn to good endings—
remarkable tension of longing
& closure, the duck's barren feet.
how skin piques like wildfowl
on a clear still lake when near one
we love—mounds of good flesh
continuing. we are a gentle breeze
from ruffling away, all goosedown
& hands laced to hold near the other
in our floating. we cling to the face of
the earth, afraid, & the wind blows.
we fly. the surface of the water prattles
then settles under holy clamor of
wings—anatidae seraphs moving to
separate, hovered on the skin of lake,
ephemeral & splitting open, creating
the whole damned world.

Ultimate Warrior's Mother

she birthed him with flamboyance   red-&-orange face-
paint in the back of a taxi   at the opera   in the eastern

service elevator of the Veedersburg Sportatorium   he barely
even cried   she held him there between the 2nd & 3rd floors

Indiana nativity   in 5th grade she pressed him
to add yellow & pink to his face   Warrior worried

other boys would laugh   she dipped a light-soaked finger
in tubs of carnation & lemon   guiding fresh color along

the line of his jaw   & when he opened his eyes   there
in the mirror was a new boy   a man's brow & chin

& all the color of heaven   Ms. Warrior smiled   her son
leaned back his head & sounded a feral yawp into the Indiana

dawn   in 10th grade he learned the Viennese waltz   bachata
the French bal-musette   by the time he graduated high school

he had fallen in love   grown skilled with fighting   taken a train
to the mountains & learned how to backcountry camp with a

waterproof pencil & cast iron for writing pastoral razor-lined odes
his mother was proud   she smiled when she spoke of his

matches in Poughkeepsie   the Spokane Coliseum
he was a good man of passion   Indiana pastel & a bench press

& a heart to drink deep the world   it is blessing that mothers
do not have to know which of their sons will die young   Indiana

pasodoble   all the fighting & the dancing   all the fragile failing
hearts   dying sons of Indiana   Indiana pietà ;

fanletters

david flanigan built the first transit cable
from the rim of zion canyon   used it
to zip lumber from the eastern
plateau woodlands to the settlers below
one can still see the mechanism today
perched atop the canyon like a burnt gull
david writes of it in letters   whisked away
by the self-same wire   up & beyond into
thin desert sky   above ranging trails
where he wrestled   with cousins   faith
low-hanging branches of limber pine

the breath of all things   wild & vinegar-full
hangs in epistles : galatians ephesians a blue-
sealed reminiscence of youth   in letters
david meditates on how a canyon
& an envelope both could seem of god
perhaps because temples can be made of
most anything   perhaps because words
stuck in a throat feel just the same as a stone
perhaps because Thy Presence inspires thought
and with thought comes regret   remorse
& suffering
                      Amen ;

for once the best option is the easiest option

it costs nothing to hold a door, to believe
that each person rootbound to the forest
floors & beaches of this odd, great world
deserves to have their hair brushed, to be told
that there is no one else quite like them in the
perfect confluence of things, that strange
happenings make for good lives—joy
& anger, school dances & silly dreams,
movie popcorn, moonbutter, heart-
ache & bluelit stars that heave soft like
sleeping rabbits, perfectly warm to touch.
for once the best option is the easiest: we
love each other as best we can in all our
failure on days we cannot bear the skin of
our own imperfect forms, we build camp
fires, sing, forgive ourselves such unlikely
blessing that we should be here now, faultless,
shrouded in grace & beautiful, making
all our mothers proud.

The Mouth of the South

age 16 : Jimmy Hart goes to his high school prom with
a girl named Viola. They eat a plate lunch at Buntyn
with a free banana pudding to share. Viola daydreams of
willow cabins, tempests that are kind, salt waves fresh in
opalescent love. They halloo their names to the reverberate hills
& dance deep in a purple evening, the only shine in Memphis
the lamps of Gaslight Square.

age 22 : Jimmy joins The Gentrys whose 1965 hit "Keep
on Dancing" would sell over a million copies with an organ
bridge as smooth as a late summer rain. He considers writing
to Viola, who he hasn't seen in years—imagines a quiet future
in a southern outback mining town, hands in the dirt & digging
pastel pieces of star.

age 35 : Jimmy comes off an Australian tour with The Beach Boys,
Sonny & Cher, Dick Clark. His high school friend, Jerry Lawler
asks him to cut a wrasslin demo. Jimmy goes on to manage, then
feud with Jerry & Ox Baker & even the song-&-dance of Andy
Kaufman. He is not a weak man, Jimmy Hart; he knows
the value of a dollar & wrestling is eight different kinds of payday.

age 42 : Jimmy signs with the WWF. He is recommended to Vince
by Hillbilly Jim, manages The Honky Tonk Man, Brutus "The Barber"
Beefcake, Money Inc., & Hulk Hogan. Wrestling is good to Jimmy.
He turns face, but never gets the same traction as when he was a
good-for-nothing scoundrel. O god give them wisdom that have it.
Still—cucullus non facit monachum.

age 51 : Jimmy goes to WCW. He manages The Giant, The
Dungeon of Doom. He feuds with Bubba the Love Sponge
& Norman Smiley. & Jimmy notices bits of growing old like
when an autumn night in Memphis seems more quiet than before
or how there once were more opals in Coober Pedy
than anywhere else in the world.

age 59 : Jimmy does the indies, TNA. He is happy with his life.
Occasionally he calls up Terry for margaritas, makes a scene or two.
& isn't that so much better than the weeping & the gnashing,
the aging self-destruction? Happiness & peace will be our story
                                        save the tears for later ;

Perry Saturn becomes the first wrestler to board the International Space Station

2 Nov 20xx   Perry was selected by a multinational team of scientists to be the first professional wrestler in orbit (the title of first in space goes to The Rock, who

travelled beyond the Kármán Line in a 3-stage Apollo-style rocket   that's 62 miles above the earth & back down again   but he never entered synchronous orbit)   As the first wrestler on the ISS   Perry pressed the boundaries of the human experience:

1.   he was the first to suplex a person in space when he performed a somewhat-shoddy crossface chickenwing suplex on Italian engineer Luca Parmitano in the Russian segment of the station

2.   he was the first to nail the technically difficult stepover armlock camel clutch in a zero-G environment on marine biologist Jessica Meir   this was doubly-impressive as Russian Oleg Skripochka had previously argued the move to be impossible without the aid of gravity

3.   he was the first person to compose a full corona of sonnets beyond the atmo boundary   it is unknown to whom they were composed or on what subject

4.   he was the first wrestler to suffer from space adaptation syndrome (SAS) also known as space sickness   which would later & more famously afflict Jerry "The King" Lawler during the second Lunar Transport Incident

by sol 14 aboard the station   Perry realizes the overwhelming divinity of his life: that here   254 mi (that's 1.341e+6 ft) above the earth, travelling a constant 4.76 mi/s (that's 17,100 mph) he can see the winter snows forming above Hokkaido 16 times per day   Perry imagines the cirrus-prayers of 7.53 bln humans drifting over the Indian Ocean   delicate icewisps in high-atmo currents of wind   Perry hears them all he knows that in 14 days his blood-forming organs have absorbed .125 Sv of radiation that the cancer-risk projection for this mission can be calculated mathematically:

$$m_J(E, a_E, a)_{lJ}(E, a_E, a) \int dL \frac{dF}{dL} LQ_{trial-J}(L)X_{L-J}$$

where dF/dL represents the folding of predictions of tissue-weighted LET spectra behind spacecraft shielding with the radiation mortality rate to form a rate for trial J on sol 19

a volcano in the Aleutian Islands erupts   Perry prepares to return to earth   somewhere in the Great Rift Valley near the soda lake Magadi a group of men harvest trona for use in making glass   Perry thinks of all the gentle things that exist under our sun

John Belk

at the top of this space elevator

at the top of this space elevator
i look across the gentle curve of the earth
horizon brought on all fours   animal spirit
& a feint of wind   orgasmed
crescendo at the top of this space elevator   i
release my grip & flutter   a silken bow
half-moonsault   a scrap of linen cloth
i drink air for breath   thin-atmosphered fish
with ribboned fins feathered toward
endless fields   a stream   a pumpkin patch &
a clump of houses warmed at the edge of a
wood   the heart unfurls like a piece of
wound wire   i will surely die   as
inevitable as this falling   i will write
my name in fish trails in a thin October sky
but O that ground that opens before
me   O that breathless flight ;

the young immortal plane
after Brian Kershisnik

here lies a buffalo   here lies a mountain of buffalo
here lies a wrestler telling stories with the soft animal
of his body
here lies a goldfinch   skinned
by the neighborhood cats

in 1872 one-point-eight million buffalo were killed
in the fields of North America
i visited once   the long grass like
swells of air released from the chest of a dream
wildreed & petrichor   tinseled heaving
of earth & sky   i bottled the wind   carried it
into the mountains with buffalo skin & a knife made of stone
i put it to sleep by the fire

& i looked for things with my tool   a saying
scry . a cotton gin & a chokehold   the barrel of a gun
in 1873 another one-point-eight million buffalo were killed
here water evaporates as prayer
here lies an ancient ocean   salt   billions
of scattered seedheads   a good story
or two   both cruel & kind   drawn from the bones of a man
the skull of a slow-moving sort of cow

Olive Saturn & the Third Plutonian Resettlement Operation

At the edge of the solar system   near the end of the third millennium
Olive Saturn writes a letter to her cousin about the polar icecaps of Charon

made ruddy by organic macromolecules as though life might simply erupt in
the crepuscular glow of the outer Orion Spur   She was born past the rim of

the Kuiper Belt   96.3 AU (that's 8.9516e+9 miles) from the sun on the Eridian
moon Dysnomia [provisional designation S/2005 (2003 UB313) 1]   Twenty-

three now   she is grown   though she still sleeps with a giraffe named
Peri that Uncle gave her the first time she visited Mars   Olive dreams

of seeing a giraffe in person   neck stretched as polyconical airseal toward the almost-
acacia-horizon   When she was five   Olive read a book from the spacebazaar

on Makemake about the Old Spanish Trail   She imagines the Great Salt Lake
to look like the tundralog fields of Charon   lightshimmer from the gasflats

guiding wagons through the the trans-Neptune tropic   a modern Polaris[3]
She imagines fields of wheat & rye   a floundering sun   a man with a whip

& a map   Peri would not have liked the mid-18th century   all its fighting
hideous glory   its stupid desire   From her pod Olive can hear the

orbital alarms of the mercantile-class dreadnought as they enter Pluto's regent-
sphere   She imagines Spanish priests crossing themselves under the stars near

Alamogordo   their prayers spun up the great neck of a giraffe   *All this space*

& we still haven't found anyone like us out here   She imagines oceans

of hurt[4]   of love   & a bright world of color   of clean chrome & yellow

& light   music playing   open armed   She imagines endless sky

---

3   The star Polaris, a navigational star, collapsed on itself during the
           second interstellar epoch.

4   In 1343 Jeanne de Clisson took her sons to witness their father's death
           before raising a Black Fleet, crimson sails full with a vengeful wind.

John Belk

The Fancy
homo sum: humani nihil a
me alienum puto

See now the hawthornes & hackberries,
pink-fruited sumacs settlers used to
make shrub or switchel or sour ginger
tea. The flesh of a quince—anointed
skin of our mothers—lures us past
the safety of the meadow, beyond
the still-quiet woods where monsters
turn & dark things fear to go. Here,
the soil refuses water. Even the devil
does not want you. We hold hands before
saying goodbye: hinc illae lacrimae. Three
leagues out in the desert & all that is
left at the end of this world is a crowd,
a fight, a last temptation, the stifled cries
of a child & all this to happen again
& again. Still,
                    what brave joys await us—
                    what shining dangerous tomorrows

Acknowledgments

"the young immortal plane" in *Jet Fuel Review*, no. 20, 2020, p. 52.
 "definition of the continental shelf" in *Jet Fuel Review*, no. 20, 2020, p. 53.

"Good Endings" in *Poetry South*, no. 12, 2020, p. 68.
 "The Fancy" in *Poetry South*, no. 12, 2020, p. 69.

"Perry Saturn makes ends meet after a failed tour with New Japan Pro Wrestling"
in *The Fourth River*, no. 9, 2020.
"At the top of this space elevator" in *The Fourth River*, no. 9, 2020.

"bar trivia: no wrestler has ever used an Annie Lennox song as entry music" in the
25th Anniversary issue of *Sport Literate*, vol. 12, no. 2 & finalist for the *Sport Literate*
25th Anniversary Prize.

"Jimmy Snuka's Mother" in *Sport Literate,* vol. 12, no. 1, Winter 2019, p. 80.
"Blackjack Mulligan's Mother" in *Sport Literate*, vol. 12, no. 1, Winter 2019, pp. 76-77.
"Angle of Regard" in *Sport Literate*, vol. 12, no. 1, Winter 2019, pp. 78-79.

Thanks

I owe thanks to so many:

To Matthew Dickman for selecting this work for the 2021 Autumn House Rising Writer award.

To Sarah Bates and Laura Walker, whose fingerprints are throughout this book.

To Mike Good and the entire Autumn House team.

To Rachel Mennies and David Kirby for their generosity and kindness.

To former teachers & mentors—Kathy O'Neal, Jan Gardner, Janet McCann, Robin Becker, Julia Kasdorf, Jim Brasfield, Todd Davis, Larry Heinemann, Cheryl Glenn.

To Kris Phillips and Lindsey Roper for rekindling my love of wrestling. To supportive colleagues and friends—Todd Petersen, Jess Tvordi, Kyle Bishop, Danielle Dubrasky, Christopher Clark, Morgaine Donohue, and so many more who have patiently humored all of the suplex and clothesline talk. To my loving partner, Cris, who has also humored all of the suplex and clothesline talk.

To Mom and Dad.

And to all the wrestlers—especially those I've spun tales about here—thank you for the stories.

May happiness and peace be yours.

New & Forthcoming Releases

Molly by Kevin Honold
Winner of the 2020 Autumn House Fiction Prize, selected by Dan Chaon

The Gardens of Our Childhoods by John Belk
Winner of the 2021 Rising Writer Prize in Poetry, selected by Matthew Dickman

Myth of Pterygium by Diego Gerard Morrison
Winner of the 2021 Rising Writer Prize in Fiction, selected by Maryse Meijer

Out of Order by Alexis Sears
Winner of the 2021 Donald Justice Poetry Prize, selected by Quincy R. Lehr

Queer Nature: A Poetry Anthology edited by Michael Walsh

Seed Celestial by Sara R. Burnett
Winner of the 2021 Autumn House Poetry Prize, selected by Eileen Myles

Bittering the Wound by Jacqui Germain
Winner of the 2021 CAAPP Book Prize, selected by Douglas Kearney

The Running Body by Emily Pifer
Winner of the 2021 Autumn House Nonfiction Prize, selected by Steve Almond

Entry Level by Wendy Wimmer
Winner of the 2021 Autumn House Fiction Prize, selected by Deesha Philyaw

For our full catalog please visit autumnhouse.org